Tall Tales: American Myths

By
Tom Lisker

A
cpi
Book

From

RAINTREE CHILDRENS BOOKS
Milwaukee • Toronto • Melbourne • London

3 4 5 6 7 8 9 0   89 88 87 86 85

Library of Congress Number: 77-11104

Art and Photo Credits

Cover illustration, Lynn Sweat
Illustrations on pages 6, 12, 16, 20, 24, 26, 29, 31, 35, 39, 40, 41, 43, 44, 47 and 48.
Jeffrey Gatrall
Every effort has been made to trace the ownership of all copyrighted material in
this book and to obtain permission for its use.

Library of Congress Cataloging in Publication Data

Lisker, Tom, 1928-
   Tall tales: American Myths

   SUMMARY: Includes the stories of Johnny Appleseed, Paul
Bunyan, Pecos Bill, and Davy Crockett and discusses how "tall tales"
started and were passed along.
   1. Tales, American. [1. Folklore—United States] 1. Title
PZ8.1.L68Ta   398.2'2'0973   77-11104
ISBN 0-8172-1039-3 lib. bdg.

Manufactured in the United States of America
ISBN 0-8172-1039-3

Contents

A SHORT WORD ABOUT TALL TALES

Chapter 1

The cowboys had bed down the herd. Dinner was long since over, and the cook joined the tired men around the lazy campfire.

"Where you 'spose we are by now?" the cook asked nobody in particular. The firelight was so low you could hardly make out their faces.

"Cookie," answered the trail boss, "I reckon we're 11, 12 days out of Laramie."

"Laramie," said Cookie. "Laramie's where I first met Pecos Bill."

5

"Have you really met Pecos Bill?" asked one of the younger cowboys, hardly believing it was possible. He thought Pecos Bill was just a hero people told stories about.

"Sure, son," said the cook, as he carefully rolled a cigarette. "I met Pecos Bill on a cattle drive just like this one. Oh, sure. Some 20, 30 years ago." Cookie reached into the fire and pulled out a glowing ember with his toughened

Tall tales helped cowboys pass the hours on long cattle drives.

fingers. The end of his cigarette blazed up in flame for a brief moment, and everyone around the campfire caught the faraway look in Cookie's eyes.

"Pecos Bill," he repeated. "Why, the first time he came into camp was early one morning, around breakfast. I'd just whipped up a batch of eggs for the men, and I offered him some. 'How about a couple of eggs, stranger?' I asked him. I didn't know who he was . . . then. 'Man,' he said, 'I don't even dirty my plate for less than a dozen!'

"Yup, he was a big feller. Strong—and smart, too! When he was just a year old, one of his sisters ran out to the field to tell Bill's daddy that a panther had just gone into the cabin where little Billy was sleeping. And Billy was all alone. 'Well,' said his daddy, 'that fool panther better not expect any help from me!' At noontime, when the Old Man finished ploughing and went back to the cabin, there was Bill cooking up panther steaks for the family. And his daddy wasn't the least bit surprised!"

On into the night Cookie told his tales of Pecos Bill. He spun yarn after yarn about the adventures of "his friend Bill." In each story, Bill

7

is a kind of super-hero. In each, he is the *biggest* eater, the *strongest* man in the West, the *most daring* of all the cowboys. Cookie was telling the kind of stories Americans love most of all—*tall tales.* You will read so many tall tales in this book, you'll wonder why the pages don't stand 12 feet high!

Tall tales are the kind of yarns New England fishermen would spin on the deck of a whaling ship to while away the time. Or they're the kind of stories the Western frontiersmen would tell, sitting around a potbellied stove drinking coffee. Tall tales are the kind of stories the cowboys would tell around a campfire. Tall tales would get even taller when a young tenderfoot or visitor from the East was curious and asked a lot of questions.

The dictionary says a tall tale is a story "difficult to believe." But some of the best tellers of tall tales will convince you the dictionary is wrong. "Tall tales," they will tell you, "are improvements only on what actually happened!" But the curious thing about tall tales is that they're never thought of as outright lies. Whoppers, perhaps—but not lies.

You must remember that when people were settling this huge country of ours, they didn't arrive from Europe or head out West with television sets for entertainment. Nor did they have radios, phonographs, or even many musical instruments. One of the main sources of entertainment during a long evening was telling stories. Fortunately for us, some pretty good listeners remembered and wrote them down.

Our tall tale heroes, like Pecos Bill, are as American as baseball, apple pie, and hot dogs—probably even more so. Let's look in on Cookie again and his stories of Pecos Bill—that famous hero of the West.

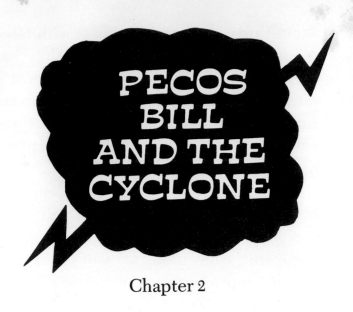

PECOS BILL AND THE CYCLONE

Chapter 2

Cookie was just getting warmed up. He knew the young cowboy no longer needed the heat of the fire even in the chilled night air. Cookie's "memories" of Pecos Bill were enough.

"You see, Bill had some of the strangest beginnings of anybody I ever met," Cookie said. "It wasn't long after he cooked up the panther steaks when his Old Man found wagon tracks about five miles from the cabin. That was a sign that things were getting too crowded in the neighborhood. Time to move.

"So he packed up the whole family, put everything in the covered wagon, and headed farther west. Just about the time they were about to cross the Pecos River, little Bill, still a tyke, jumped out of the wagon. It wasn't 'til days later they noticed he was gone. They knew it had been kinda *quiet*, but Bill always was a heavy sleeper.

"Bill's Mom was afraid for Bill. I mean he was among the wild animals and poisonous rattlers. But the Old Man kept saying, 'Those varmints and rattlers will have to fend for themselves.'

"Meanwhile, as Bill told me, he toddled around and finally found himself a pack of coyotes. He fought and whipped every last one of them to show who was boss. Then he taught them everything he knew and learned from them everything they knew.

"By the time Bill was grown up, he could talk in all the animal languages. He could smell a trail, run with the pack, and forecast the weather. The only problem was *he thought he was a coyote*!

"Actually, it wasn't a problem at all until a cowboy named Bowleg Gerber—he's the one brought Bill into town—saw Bill leaping around the range stark naked making coyote noises.

Pecos Bill was raised by a coyote pack and became their leader.

"They had this fierce argument. Bill sayin' he was a coyote, and Bowleg askin' how could he be without a bushy tail. Bill showed him his fleas, and Bowleg said it didn't mean nothin'. 'All Texans got fleas!' When Bowleg showed Bill his reflection in the river, Bill finally realized, much to his disappointment, that he was a human being, and not a coyote at all."

Cookie flipped the tail end of his cigarette into the fire, which by now was so low that it was just red, glowing coals.

"Is that the end?" asked the young cowboy.

"Well, no," sighed the cook, as he leaned back on a blanket roll. "It's more like the beginning, because Pecos Bill (called that because he was lost near the Pecos River) decided to become a cowboy, just like you."

"Just like me? Golly," said the young tenderfoot, as bright-eyed as the coals in the fire.

"Bowleg showed up with a horse and whip for Bill—told him he'd need 'em to get a job as a cowboy. But, by that time, Bill had an animal already. He pointed to a huge panther he had just trained to ride. Then he lifted a sort of peaceful looking rattlesnake—he'd trained it for a whip.

"Bowleg and Bill rode into camp, the most unlikely looking partners you'd ever want to see. It wasn't long—about a minute or two—when Pecos Bill became boss of the outfit. He'd been boss of the coyotes so long, it just seemed natural.

"Being a cowboy then wasn't much like being a cowboy now. Bill changed a lot of it, you know. He invented herding, and branding, and cattle drives, and singing to cattle. Lots of folks say Mr. Anonymous made up songs like 'Bury Me

Not' and 'Git Along Little Doggie' but the cow-punchers know Pecos Bill made up the best of them."

"Gosh," said the young cowboy, "what *didn't* he do?"

Cookie coughed, cleared his throat, looked around at the other cowboys for a moment, and then continued. "Funny thing about Bill. He did most everything. You wonder sometimes what things would have been like today if he'd just stayed a coyote. One of the things he invented, just as an example, is the six-shooter. He was also the first man to tame a wild horse. Up 'til then, cowboys rode ponies. Can you imagine? A cow-boy on a *pony*? He also invented the lariat. He did everything at least once!"

The trail boss leaned forward and asked in his hoarse voice, "Cookie, did you see the time he busted the cyclone?"

"I sure did. Never forget it, neither. That was the year of the Great Drought. In fact, that's what made him bust the cyclone."

The trail boss stood up and scratched behind his right ear and said, "I never did see Pecos Bill, but I remember the Great Drought. That was somethin'! The ground got so hard that if you wanted to plant a crop, you had to shoot seeds into it with a six-shooter. Otherwise, they'd never get in there. Too hard to dig. Got so dry without water that the cattle's tongues drooped out far 'nuff we were afraid they'd trip on them. I tell ya, it was *dry*.

"Seemed that people would get so dried out their faces were like sandpaper. Just about everybody was pulling up stakes to head West, except Uncle Luke. He held out, figuring it was going to rain one day. He thought he might just as well wait there as anyplace else.

"Uncle Luke sat on his rickety old front porch. It was the only place with shade, except for inside the cabin. Without a breeze, it got to around 150 degrees in there. Even the flies fell over from heat exhaustion. Uncle Luke was pretty handy with the harmonica, so he'd sit there and play ditties while waitin' for the rain.

"One day, he started playing 'Stars and Stripes Forever,' which he could do real well. All of a sudden, he looked down at his feet. Down there, right by his rocker, stood the biggest, meanest, diamondback rattler he'd ever seen.

Uncle Luke and the rattler, J.P., made beautiful music together.

This rattler looked just as pleased, sitting there and rocking to the music. Uncle Luke was so scared he near swallowed his harmonica. It's a good thing he didn't, because this rattler was a music lover.

"The rattler swayed back and forth to everything Luke played, and you can bet he kept on playin'. He played every tune he knew—all the ditties that Pecos Bill wrote. Pretty soon he was back to 'Stars and Stripes Forever.' Well, sir, that's the tune the rattlesnake liked best for sure.

He swayed right in time—in fact, he started shaking his rattles to the music, and it made a right pretty sound.

"By this time, Uncle Luke was so plumb tuckered and out of breath from blowing his harmonica that he turned blue. He figured he'd just as soon be eaten up by the rattler as die of harmonica blowin'. So he stopped. Well, when he did, just as you please, the rattler slithered off into the hard-packed fields.

"Same thing happened the next day. And darned if the rattler didn't show his real pleasure for 'Stars and Stripes Forever.' Before you knew it, the rattler was coming every day and really perking up to the song. Uncle Luke even gave him a name—J.P., short for John Philip Sousa, the man who wrote 'Stars and Stripes Forever.'

"Well, just as Uncle Luke predicted, the rains finally came and things started getting better. It wasn't long before old Luke's place was one of the richest grazing lands in the territory. Only problem was he hadn't seen old J.P., the rattler, since the rains came. He looked for him all right. He played 'Stars and Stripes Forever' all hours of the day and night, but no J.P.

"One day, Jeff Brainerd, who owned over 100 head of cattle to the south, was looking to rent some pastureland for his herd. He came by Uncle Luke's. They set off in the buckboard to the north to see the rich grazing property and watering spots.

"As they were bouncing along, the sound of music was floating down over the prairie. It was coming from a nearby hill. The buckboard could never make that hill in a million years. So Uncle Luke bounded out and raced up the hill on his wobbly old legs. There on the top, the strangest sight he ever did see met his eyes. Right there, on a big flat rock were 28 big, diamondback rattlers in one big huge circle. In the center, his head swaying proudly, was old J.P. Sousa, leading them all in a rousing round of 'Stars and Stripes Forever'."

"Wow!" said the young cowboy. "That's really something. But what happened to Pecos Bill in the Great Drought?"

"Well, son," said Cookie. "Pecos Bill ended it single-handed."

"What do you mean?"

"You see, the Great Drought was a terrible, terrible thing. Animals were dying from lack of

18

water. People were leaving the West—there was nothing left for them to do. And Pecos Bill was very upset. He went riding around on his favorite horse, Widow Maker, until he got an idea. And when it came to him he went right into action.

"He set off on some hard riding all over Texas and into Oklahoma. Once he got into Oklahoma, he spotted just what he was looking for. There was thunder and a big black funnel in the sky, with lightning on its edges. It was a real, full-blown cyclone!

"When he figured he was close enough, he swung his lariat, which was only about 200 miles shorter than the equator. He lassoed the cyclone right around its neck.

"The fiercer the cyclone fought, the more the lariat tightened around the neck. Bill held on 'til just the right moment when he could leap on it. Well, the cyclone gave a snort you could hear for three states, and it started using all the tricks of a buckin' bronco. But Bill hung on, slapping the cyclone with his *sombrero* and diggin' in with his spurs.

"He was determined to ride it out, and he rode that bucking cyclone all over Oklahoma,

When the Great Drought was in the West, Pecos Bill just lassoed a cyclone and watered the land.

New Mexico, and on into Texas. When he got to the areas that were parched with drought, the cyclone did just what Pecos Bill had figured. It rained right out from under him. And that's how thousands of cattle and people were saved from dying of thirst.

"Naturally, when Bill slid down a streak of lightning, he suffered a mild discomfort. His horse, Widow Maker, found her way home from Oklahoma three days later, and everything returned to normal."

"How did Pecos Bill ever find Widow Maker in the first place?" asked the tenderfoot cowboy. But by then the cowhands were all standing, stretching, and yawning. It was getting very late, and they were ready to climb into their sleeping rolls and call it a night.

"Some other night, young feller," said a cowboy kindly. "We'll even tell you about Sweet Sue, and how Bill lassoed her down from the crescent of the moon."

Chapter 3

Pecos Bill and his friends would talk mostly about rattlesnakes, cattle, and heat. Paul Bunyan and the people he lived with were more concerned with huge trees, tremendous amounts of hotcakes, and very, very cold weather. One winter, the temperature got to about 200—300 degrees below zero. Now, that kind of cold can make some strange things happen. For one thing, plain smoke from a fire will *freeze*!

That kind of weather is cold enough to freeze the entire Pacific Ocean, which it did one year.

The only trouble was it got so cold so fast, there wasn't any snow for people to sleighride on. So Paul Bunyan and Babe, his Blue Ox, scooted across the frozen Pacific Ocean to China to pick up a load of snow and haul it back to Minnesota. But we're getting way ahead of the story.

Who was Paul Bunyan? Where did he come from? Well . . . he was actually big enough at birth to be born in several places. When he was just three weeks old, Paul caused his family some trouble by kicking his little baby feet around and knocking down about four miles of trees. Since this happened in the state of Maine, most folks tend to think Paul Bunyan was born there. But, as we said, he was big enough so it could have been several states. The people in Maine did ask Paul's family, very nicely, of course, if they'd please move him to some other place where he'd do less damage.

The family made Paul a cradle out of the timber he'd knocked over, and they anchored it off the Maine coast. But you know babies. Pretty soon, Paul started waving his arms and legs, you know, the way babies do. Well, that started the cradle rocking, which then started a whole bunch of waves which came pounding down on the

23

Paul, as a young babe, created some special problems
for his parents.

seashore. Those waves were so high, they almost
flooded every town along the New England coast.

You can probably see by now that Paul
Bunyan was a rather large fellow. During the next
few years, Paul had to learn how to move about
without hurting people. He even decided to in-
vent logging. Of course, he had already invented
hunting and fishing, as we now know.

Logging was very slow work until Paul set his mind to changing things. Just for example, do you know how the loggers used to keep their axes sharp? They'd go to the top of a hill, where they'd find a big stone. They'd roll this stone down the hill, and the logger would hold the axe blade edge on the stone as he ran alongside of it.

Paul could see right off that this method of sharpening a blade would work fine if the stone was nice and round and the hill was nice and smooth. But most often they weren't. So he invented the grindstone, and that saved the loggers a lot of running.

To increase production, he invented the two-man saw. In his case it really should have been called the "eight-man saw." That's because when he was pulling on one end, it would take seven normal-sized men at the other end to keep up with him.

The roads leading into the woods were always very narrow, and there was never enough room for a four-horse team to turn around to face in the opposite direction. The loggers would fell the trees and then load them on the flat, wooden sleds. But they had no way to go backwards. To turn around, they'd have to wait for Paul to come by. He would lift the four horses and the load and place them in the right direction. Since that was wasting time and cutting down production, Paul invented the loop turn in the road. After that, turning around didn't waste any more time.

There were always many animals in camp, but Babe, the Blue Ox, was the biggest and most useful. He was also Paul's favorite. Babe was born in the Winter of the Blue Snow, which is why he was sky blue. But his nose was black and his horns were pure white. He measured over 42 axe handles between those horns, and he could eat in one day all the feed you could haul into camp in a year.

The road wasn't wide enough for the horses to turn. Paul just lifted the horses and turned them around.

You know that to move a whole slew of logs, the easiest and best way is to float them down a river. Well, some days Babe would get it in his head to sneak up behind a crew and drink up a river. Then the logs would be sitting high and dry in the mud and couldn't be budged. That was bothersome.

But Babe was always more of a help than a bother. There was that one winding stretch of road between these two towns in Wisconsin. As the crow flies, it was only about 20 or so miles, but it was much longer on the winding road. Paul Bunyan hitched Babe to the road, and after a good share of huffing and puffing, Babe stretched that road out straight. In fact, once the road was straight between the towns, they had 53 extra miles of road they couldn't use. Paul *did* do something with those extra miles, but nobody remembers what.

One of the biggest problems in a lumber camp is feeding all the men. It seems that there's nothing a lumberjack likes so much as hotcakes. Paul's cousin Joe, the cook, was the only man ever to be able to make hotcakes fast enough for Paul and his crew.

One of the first things Joe did was to get Ole the Blacksmith to make a big enough griddle. It was so huge you couldn't see across it on a foggy day. To stir the batter, he got a couple of dozen cement mixers. And to keep the griddle greased, Joe hired a team of men who went skating across it with slabs of bacon tied to their feet. This way, the hotcakes could come fast enough for the 462 assistant cooks to cart them to the men.

Paul found himself a wife who was very young, but she eventually grew up to his size. They had two children, Teeny and Jean. Teeny was very smart. She was the one who figured out what to do when the hens couldn't lay their eggs fast enough to keep up with the supply of hot-cakes. What she did was to plant a great big eggplant on top of a mountain, some 50 miles from camp. She'd roll the eggs from the eggplant right down the mountain and into camp. That way, the eggs would all be beaten and ready for cooking by the time they arrived.

Probably the most important and world fa-mous thing that ever happened to Paul Bunyan was when he got the letter from the King of Sweden. Ole the Blacksmith read it for him, be-cause it came written in Swedish, with a royal seal and everything. It seems that Sweden was get-ting very crowded, and the king asked Paul if he could find some room for the extra Swedes in America.

Paul had the idea that North Dakota would be a perfect spot, but first he had to clear all the timber so they could farm the land. He began the biggest logging adventure in all of history. Thousands and thousands of men helped Paul clear North Dakota. You could hear "Tim-ber" in neighboring states and even up in Canada.

Of course, feeding a crew that large was almost impossible, but Paul figured out a way. There was this big lake a few miles from camp. Every so often Paul would fill it up with green

Clearing all the timber from the state of North Dakota sure built up healthy appetites. So Paul prepared a lake full of pea soup.

peas and throw in a half dozen pigs for soup stock. After a wagon load of salt, he'd pile logs all along the shore and set fire to it. When the soup started to boil, he'd have six or seven cooks paddle around in rowboats, keeping everything all nicely stirred up. Then he'd pipe the soup down to camp at mealtime. You could actually turn the soup on or off with this big faucet.

Of course, hotcakes were delivered on horseback to the longest tables ever built. Paul invented roller skates and he taught all the cooks and servers to use them. That man even had special teams of salt and pepper wagons that would ride up and down the tables. Each round trip would take about two days, if you kept a pretty good pace.

Things went very well for Paul and his crew. They cut so much timber that their stacks of logs got higher and higher. It took most of the day just to get around one pile of logs, so Paul built the Big Sawmill. He also put Shot Gunderson in charge of floating the rest of the logs down the Mississippi River to St. Louis. Everybody was so amazed at the huge number of logs floating down the river, they forgot all about St. Louis and didn't stop 'til they reached clear down to New Orleans.

Babe was good and thirsty so he drank enough of the Mississippi to make it run upstream.

When Paul heard about it, he could hardly stop laughing. But, as usual, he thought of a simple solution.

He got Babe thirsty and drove him over to the upper Mississippi to drink. When Babe started drinking to get rid of his huge thirst, the Mississippi, believe it or not, started to run up stream! Mark Twain was going to mention this fact in one of his books, but he ran out of room.

Naturally, they were able to float the logs right back up the Mississippi, and this time they remembered to stop at St. Louis.

Pretty soon, North Dakota was cleared, and Paul invited the King of Sweden to take a look. Once the King saw all the tree stumps that the loggers had left, he told Paul his people couldn't possibly farm land in that condition. So Paul took a big sledgehammer and drove down each and every stump at least six feet underground. That's why you see so few stumps in North Dakota. And even to this day, if you were to look around in North Dakota, you'd find lots of Swedish families still living there.

JOHNNY
APPLESEED-
THE
APPLESEED
PLANTER

Chapter 4

Now perhaps you've heard folks talk from time to time about a man named Johnny Appleseed. He was different from Pecos Bill and Paul Bunyan because we have a lot more real written facts about Johnny. First off, his name wasn't always Johnny Appleseed. It was John Chapman. You can look that up in the records of the year 1775, more or less, in the city of Boston, Massachusetts. Or maybe it was Ipswich. Anyway, it's right there in the records.

The day John Chapman was born happened to be a rainy one in May. When the sun came out all bright and perky, the nurse took Johnny to the window to see his first rainbow. This beautiful rainbow curved right down into the Chapman backyard and touched the apple tree, which was loaded with blossoms. The rainbow colored all those blossoms in such a way that Johnny bounced and gurgled and reached out as if he wanted to pick the blossoms. And that little boy was only 40 minutes old!

Some people don't believe this story, but it's a known fact that, as a baby, Johnny would never give anybody a moment's peace until he had a branch of apple blossoms to sniff.

After college, Johnny and his family moved to Pennsylvania. Something happened there that had a lasting effect on him. It didn't change him, really. He just became . . . . *different.*

Some folks say something happened to Johnny when a woman broke her promise to marry him. Others say he caught malaria, and that it did something to his mind. Others believe he was kicked in the head by a horse he was doctoring. But whatever the real truth is, Johnny decided in Pennsylvania what his "mission" would be. He decided to plant apple trees all over the Middle West. And that's just what he did.

Every fall, during cider making time, he would collect the mashed-up pulp left over after the juice had been squeezed out of the apples. Then he'd pick out the seeds, thousands and thousands of them, fill his leather pouches, and head off to Ohio and Indiana.

If a family was heading west, he'd give them little packets of apple seeds. The big bundles, though, he'd carry himself. He'd stop along rich riverbanks and meadows and plant apple trees where there weren't any people.

Johnny's "mission" was to make the land bloom with apple trees.

Even after the seedlings got started, Johnny Appleseed, as people started to call him, would stop by to tend them. As the years passed, he traveled as far south as Tennessee and as far west as the Rocky Mountains. He'd eat whatever was handy and sleep out in the open. Johnny made friends all across the wilderness.

Johnny never carried a gun, or even a knife. Only once did he ever kill a living thing—a rattlesnake that bit him. He was sad every time he remembered the incident.

Johnny did have a strange look to him, though. His hair, which eventually turned gray, hung loosely about his shoulders down to his chest. His beard waved in the breeze. His shirt was an old coffee sack or sugar bag, with holes cut out for his head and his arms. One single, tired suspender held his pants up. The pants themselves were shredded just below the knee. His hat, when he wore one, was the pot he cooked his vittles in. According to the folks who'd seen him, he'd usually be heading a parade of animals and birds wherever he went.

Johnny probably didn't know it, but he *did* cause some problems that still exist even now in Ohio. He somehow got it into his head that dog fennel, a very smelly kind of weed, would prevent the dreaded disease, malaria. So he planted it all over the country. It turns out that dog fennel, or May weed, as it's known in some places, doesn't prevent malaria at all. Just about all it does is grow fast and smell bad. Some folks think that Johnny planted it all over as a joke on the farmers, but that probably isn't true.

Here's something else that's the truth. You can look it up if you want. When Senator Sam Houston of Texas heard that Johnny Appleseed had died, he stood up and made a speech in Washington. Toward the end he said, "This old man was a great citizen. His was a work of love, and in time people will call him blessed."

Now, in your lifetime, you're going to read and hear about many heroes, but none will be more important than Davy Crockett. He's important to know because he was part of American history. In fact, if you look in the Capitol in Washington, D.C., you'll see the very spot that old Davy had his desk when he was in Congress.

DAVY
CROCKETT
KING OF
THE OLD
WILD
WEST

Chapter 5

Davy Crockett was a member of the U.S. House of Representatives from 1827-31 and from 1833-35. Of course, nobody thought he would be that important when he first grew up in Tennessee. He lived in a cabin just like all the people in the area. All those homes looked the same, but you can believe they were different. You see, Davy's mother, even when she was an old lady, could jump a seven rail fence backwards. She could spin more wool than a steam mill and cut down a gum tree and sail it across the Nolachuky River, using her apron for a sail.

Davy's mother was a very unusual woman. Jumping a seven rail fence backwards was no problem for her.

When he was born, Davy was given a cradle 12 feet long. His voice was so loud, he'd set the cider barrels rolling around in the cellar. They had to hang his cradle high on the very top of a tree so the breeze could swing it about.

Davy Crockett ate a big meal for a young boy. He drank buffalo milk and polished off a whole duck just to get started. Then he'd finish with big helpings of bear meat.

Davy rode on the back of his sheepdog, Butcher, and learned how to shoot a bow and arrow and how to throw a tomahawk by the time he was three. On his eighth birthday, he weighed 200 pounds.

When he was old enough to own a gun, the men in the district taught Davy everything they knew about shooting. Then he added some new

His sheepdog, Butcher, helped Davy to get from place to place.

When the family needed food, Davy never failed at hunting.

rules of his own. One was, "Be sure you're right, and then go ahead and pull the trigger."

They tell a story about a time when Davy had many chores to do and little time for hunting. The family needed some food, so he figured he'd do some fast hunting.

It wasn't long before he saw a flock of geese and a big buck. Just when he was about to shoot, he noticed a rattlesnake ready to strike. He shot the buck with one barrel and took the flock of geese with the other. They were all in line, of course, every one of them. Then, in one quick motion, he jammed the ramrod down the snake's throat.

At the same time, Davy's gun had such a kick, it knocked him into the river. When he climbed out, every pocket was full of fish. They were so heavy, two of his coat buttons popped off. One button hit and killed a bear, and the other knocked over a squirrel.

Even the *animals* in the territory knew Davy was the best shot around. Folks tell the story about a raccoon who was sitting quietly in a tree when Davy came by. Davy was carrying Brown Bess, his favorite gun, over his shoulder. The raccoon spotted him, lifted his paw and said, "Hey, wait a minute. You're Davy Crockett, aren't you?" Davy said he was one and the same, and the raccoon said that he'd come right down. He'd heard Davy was the finest shot in the land.

Davy was flattered by the comments of the raccoon. He thanked the animal, patted him on the head, and said he wouldn't hurt a hair on him. "Don't mind if I leave," said the raccoon. "It's not

The raccoon recognized Davy and came down from the tree.

that I doubt your word, but I thought I'd get going just in case you change your mind."

Davy Crockett got married and had a family that could out-run, out-jump, and out-scream just about any family in Tennessee. He tamed wild animals to help him and the family with the chores.

Davy was a great animal trainer. He once trained a wolf so well that if anybody was cold, the wolf would shiver for them. Davy trained a panther to light a path in the dark with just the fire in the panther's eyes. People swear they watched that same animal clean off the front porch with his tail. Then they watched the panther rake the garden with his claws.

The panther took care of many chores such as sweeping the porch and raking the garden.

The prize animal around the Crockett farm was the tame bear, Death Hug. On Sundays, he carried Davy's daughter's pocketbook to church with the money for the collection plate in his mouth. Davy taught him to smoke a pipe and many other things, too.

One thing about Davy was that he always kept his promises. That, plus the fact that he was the world's greatest storyteller (mostly about himself as the hero), probably made him a Congressman. "I can out-speak any man," said Davy, and that was the truth.

Poor Davy got himself killed, as you probably know, at the Alamo in 1837. But you can look that up, too.

A
FINAL
WORD

Chapter 6

Of course, Johnny Appleseed passed away in
1845. We don't know the year that Pecos Bill
died, but we know it was when he saw a man from
Boston in a mail-order cowboy outfit. Meanwhile, nobody knows for sure what happened to
Paul Bunyan.

That just about takes care of everybody we
talked about. But you've got to believe there are a
lot more. There's Jonathan Slick, Windwagon
Smith, Feboldson and Bridges, and Joe Magarac,
just to name a few. And if you'd like to read more

tall tales, you'll find some beauties about John Henry, Mike Fink, and Captain Stormalong. We'd like to tell you about them all, but we just kinda ran out of room.

Pecos Bill just laughed himself to death when he saw a man from Boston in a mail-order cowboy suit.

The Saturday Review of Literature is a fine magazine. It once said about tall tales in America, "We are guilty of telling tall tales, yes—but we have made many a tall tale *dream* come true." And that's the truth. You can look it up.